For Ben, with much love — FW

For Sue — RBC

BLOOMSBURY
CHILDREN'S
BOOKS

First published in Great Britain in 2001 by Bloomsbury Publishing Plc
38 Soho Square, London W1D 3HB

Individual copyright details feature on the acknowledgements page situated at the back of this book
Selection copyright © Fiona Waters 2001
Illustrations copyright © Robin Bell Corfield 2001
The moral right of the author and illustrator has been asserted.

A CIP catalogue record for this book is available from the British Library.
ISBN 0 7475 5085 9

Designed by Dawn Apperley

Printed and bound in Malaysia

1 3 5 7 9 10 8 6 4 2

Fire and Stone, Wind and Tide
Poems about the Elements

Fiona Waters and Robin Bell Corfield

BLOOMSBURY
CHILDREN'S
BOOKS

Contents

The Spinning Earth

The earth, they say,
spins round and round.
It doesn't look it
from the ground,
and never makes
a spinning sound.

And water never
swirls and swishes
from oceans full
of dizzy fishes,
and shelves don't lose
their pans and dishes.

And houses don't go whirling by
or puppies swirl around the sky.
Or robins spin instead of fly.

It may be true
what people say
about one spinning
night and day ...
But I keep wondering, anyway.

AILEEN FISHER

Earth Song

It's an earth song —
And I've been waiting long
For an earth song.
It's a spring song!
I've been waiting long
For a spring song:

Strong as the bursting of young buds,
Strong as the shoots of a new plant,
Strong as the coming of the first child
From its mother's womb —

An earth song!
A body song!
A spring song!
And I've been waiting long
For an earth song.

LANGSTON HUGHES

The Earth and the People

The earth was here before the people.
The very first people
came out of the ground.
Everything came from the ground,
even caribou.
Children once grew
out of the ground
just as flowers do.
Women out wandering
found them sprawling on the grass
and took them home and nursed them.
That way people multiplied.

This land of ours
has become habitable
because we came here
and learned how to hunt.

TRADITIONAL INUIT SONG

11

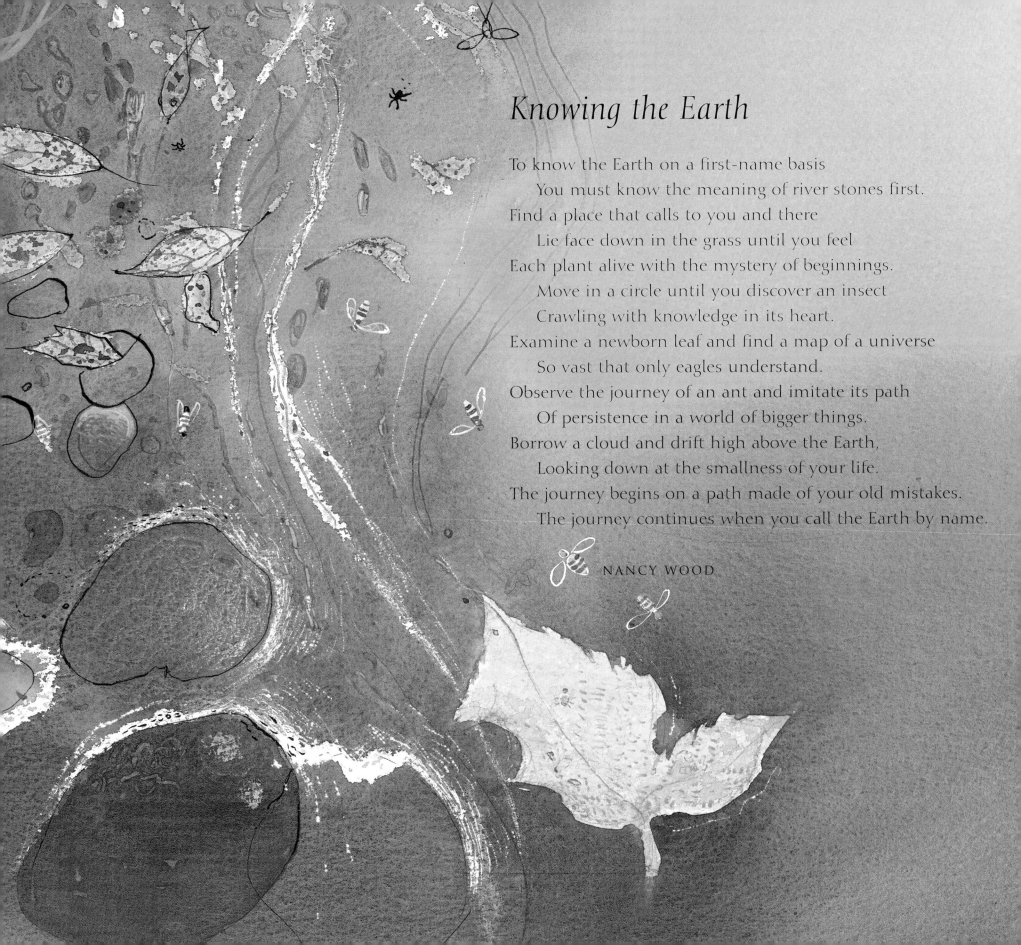

Knowing the Earth

To know the Earth on a first-name basis
 You must know the meaning of river stones first.
Find a place that calls to you and there
 Lie face down in the grass until you feel
Each plant alive with the mystery of beginnings.
 Move in a circle until you discover an insect
 Crawling with knowledge in its heart.
Examine a newborn leaf and find a map of a universe
 So vast that only eagles understand.
Observe the journey of an ant and imitate its path
 Of persistence in a world of bigger things.
Borrow a cloud and drift high above the Earth,
 Looking down at the smallness of your life.
The journey begins on a path made of your old mistakes.
 The journey continues when you call the Earth by name.

NANCY WOOD

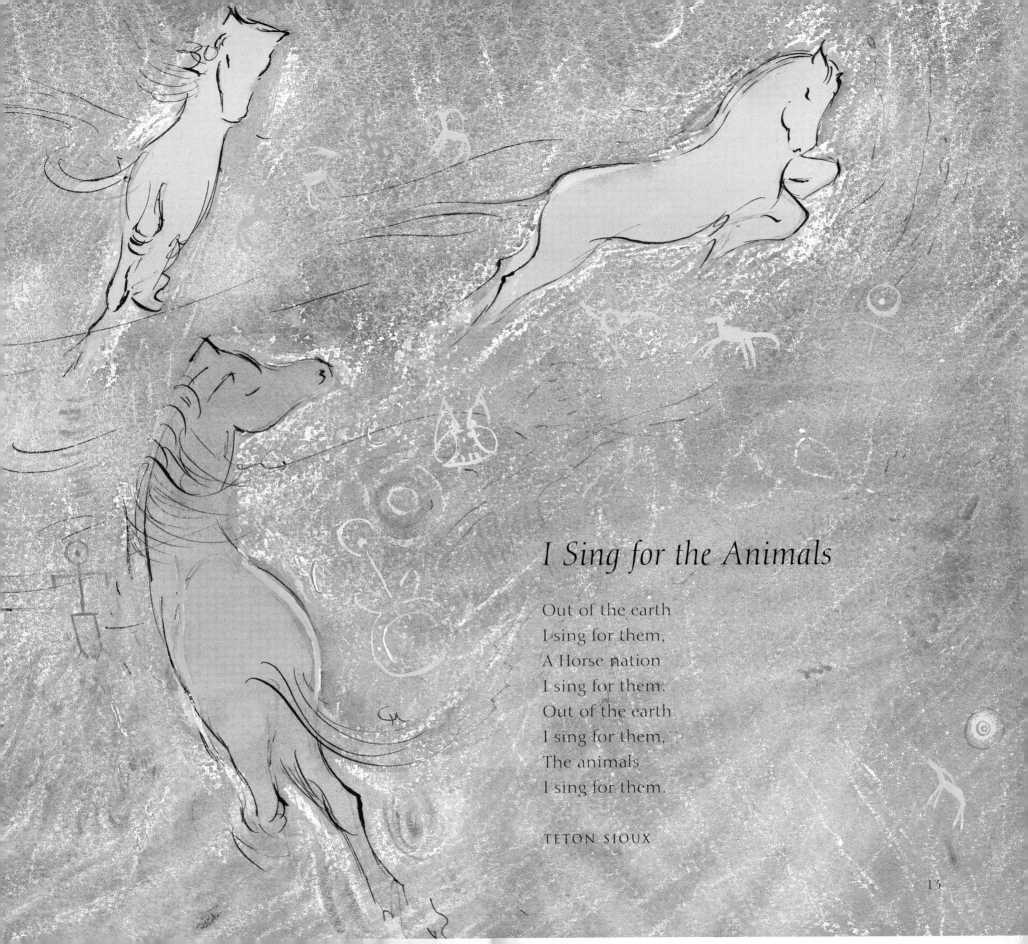

I Sing for the Animals

Out of the earth
I sing for them,
A Horse nation
I sing for them.
Out of the earth
I sing for them,
The animals
I sing for them.

TETON SIOUX

13

The World

Great, wide, beautiful, wonderful World,
With the wonderful water round you curled,
And the wonderful grass upon your breast —
World, you are beautifully dressed.

The wonderful air is over me,
And the wonderful wind is shaking the tree,
It walks on the water, and whirls the mills,
And talks to itself on the tops of the hills.

You friendly Earth, how far do you go,
With the wheatfields that nod and the rivers that flow,
With cities and gardens, and cliffs, and isles,
And people upon you for thousands of miles?

Ah, you are so great, and I am so small,
I tremble to think of you, World, at all;
And yet, when I said my prayers today,
A whisper inside me seemed to say,
'You are more than the Earth, though you are such a dog:
You can love and think, and the Earth cannot.'

WILLIAM BRIGHTY RANDS

I Like the World

I like the world
The world is good
World of water
World of wood
World of feather
World of bone
World of mountain
World of stone.

World of fibre
World of spark
World of sunshine
World of dark
World of raindrop
World of dew
World of me
and
World of you.

STEVE TURNER

Finders-Keepers, Losers-Weepers

Men once found ways to share with Earth,
To give and take in equal worth,
Then passed her on for us to keep.
If we lose her, who'll be here to weep?

PAT MOON

17

On Looking into the Grand Canyon

The Colorado chuckles —
Me, I'd laugh.
Knowing I was strong enough
To slice the world in half.

RICHARD EDWARDS

Be Ready

Be land ready
for you shall go back to land.

Be sea ready
for you have been nine-tenths water
and the salt taste shall cling to your mouth.

Be sky ready
for air, air, been so needful to you —
you shall go back, back to the sky.

CARL SANDBURG

The Wind is a Man with a Spade in His Hand

The wind is a man with a spade in his hand.
He stands above the earth and shovels the winds.
He shovels the winds into the south,
and the winds that blow into the north.
He shovels the winds to the east and to the west.

TRADITIONAL LAPLAND

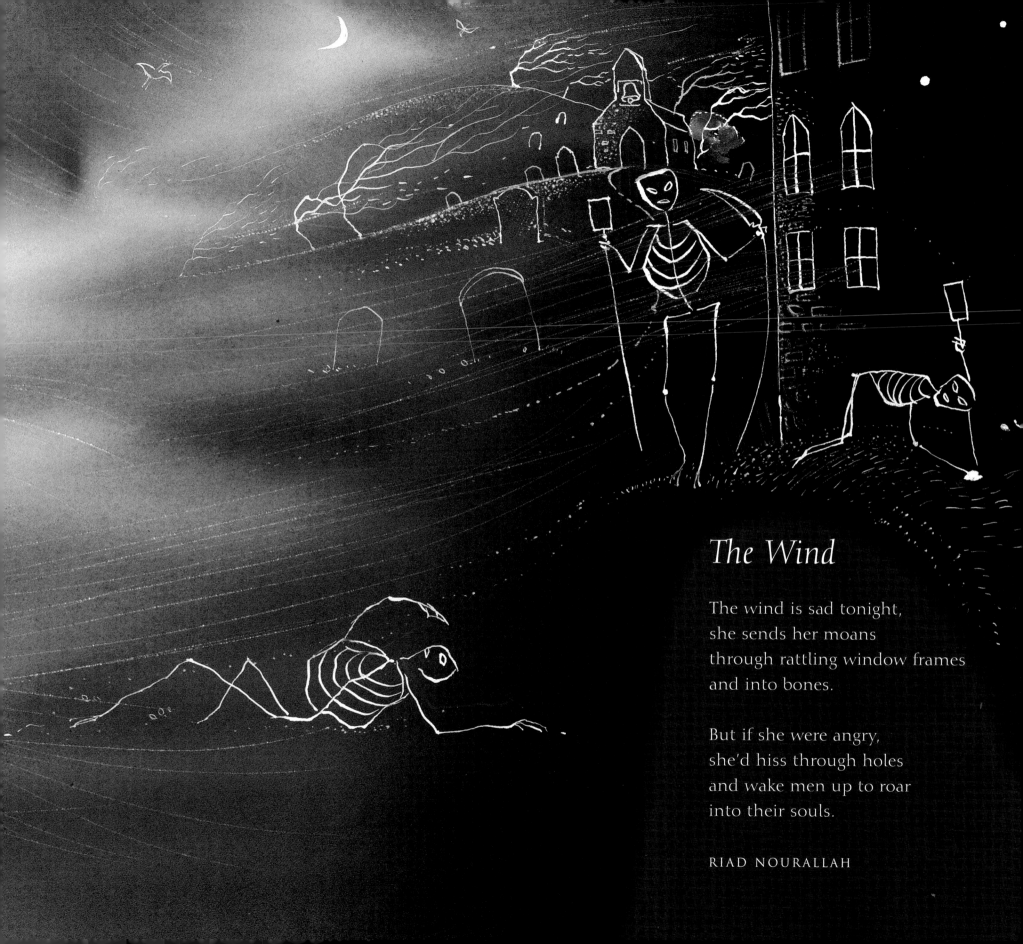

The Wind

The wind is sad tonight,
she sends her moans
through rattling window frames
and into bones.

But if she were angry,
she'd hiss through holes
and wake men up to roar
into their souls.

RIAD NOURALLAH

Who Has Seen the Wind?

Who has seen the wind?
Neither I nor you:
But when the leaves hang trembling
The wind is passing through.

Who has seen the wind?
Neither you nor I:
But when the trees bow down their heads
The wind is passing by.

CHRISTINA ROSSETTI

The Wind

The wind is a dog
flattening all this tall grass
before lying down.

KEVIN HART

Wind Cat

Jeoffrey will not go out tonight,
Hovers by the cat-flap, paw uplifted,
Eyes wide and wild ears pricked
Listening to wind-cat prowling the earth.

Wind-cat assaults the cat-flap violently
With invisible paws,
But does not come in,
Does not have a smell,
But spits savagely in Jeoffrey's face,
Then retires to leap through the garden
Tearing and smashing fearsomely

At Jeoffrey's trees,
Making Jeoffrey's fence
Creak violently;
Transmitting his terrible size,
Then is back, rattling the flap,
Spitting again, a fearsome show.

Yet Jeoffrey
Is not entirely convinced,
How can so great a creature have no smell
But the usual grass, earth and trees?
Jeoffrey suspects a con
Until the cat next door,
The usual cat-flap burglar,
Terror of the road,
Streaks past the window
Cowering to the earth,
Soaked, blown and beaten
By the wind-cat's paws.

Jeoffrey seems to shrug,
Retires to the lounge
To wash, by the fire
And guard the house against
An infinitely smaller wind-cat
Burgling down the chimney.
He knows his limitations,
That's his strength.

ROBERT WESTALL

25

I Do Not Mind You, Winter Wind

I do not mind you, Winter Wind
when you come whirling by,
to tickle me with snowflakes
drifting softly from the sky.

I do not even mind you
when you nibble at my skin,
scrambling over all of me
attempting to get in. But when you bowl me over
and I land on my behind,
then I must tell you, Winter Wind,
I mind … I really mind!

JACK PRELUTSKY

Sun

The sun
Is a leaping fire
Too hot
To go near,

But it will still
Lie down
In warm yellow squares
On the floor

Like a flat
Quilt, where
The cat can curl
And purr.

VALERIE WORTH

Firefly

On a June night
I once saw
a small dart of fire
burning in the honeysuckle bush,
flashing, flickering,
then flying slow and low
in the darkening world.

CHARLOTTE ZOLOTOW

Fire

What is it that shoots from the mountains so high,
    In many a beautiful spire?
What is it that blazes and curls to the sky?
    This beautiful something is fire.

Loud noises are heard in the caverns to groan,
    Hot cinders fall thicker than snow;
Huge stones to a wonderful distance are thrown,
    For burning fire rages below.

When winter blows bleak, and loud bellows the storm,
    And frostily twinkle the stars;
Then bright burns the fire in the chimney so warm,
    And the kettle sings shrill on the bars.

ANN TAYLOR

30

Lighting a Fire

One quick scratch
Of a kitchen match
And giant flames unzip!

How do they store
So huge a roar
In such a tiny tip?

X J KENNEDY

Firelight

Last night
as flames curled round my coal
I thought I saw
a million years ago
a forest fall.

JUDITH NICHOLLS

When We Come Home, Blake Calls for Fire

Fire, you handsome creature, shine.
Let the hearth where I confine
your hissing tongues that rise and fall
be the home that warms us all.

When the wind assaults my doors
every corner's cold but yours.
When the snow puts earth to sleep
let your bright behaviour keep

all these little pilgrims warm.
They who never did you harm
raise their paws a little higher
and toast their toes, in praise of fire.

NANCY WILLARD

The Castle in the Fire

The andirons were the dragons,
    Set out to guard the gate
Of the old enchanted castle,
    In the fire upon the grate.

We saw a turret window
    Open a little space,
And frame, for just a moment,
    A lady's lovely face;

Then, while we watched in wonder
    From out the smoky veil,
A gallant knight came riding,
    Dressed in coat of mail;

With slender lance a-tilting,
    Thrusting with a skillful might,
He charged the crouching dragons —
    Ah, 'twas a brilliant fight!

Then, in the roar and tumult,
    The back log crashed in two,
And castle, knight and dragons
    Were hidden from our view;

But, when the smoke had lifted,
    We saw, to our delight,
Riding away together,
    The lady and the knight.

MARY JANE CARR

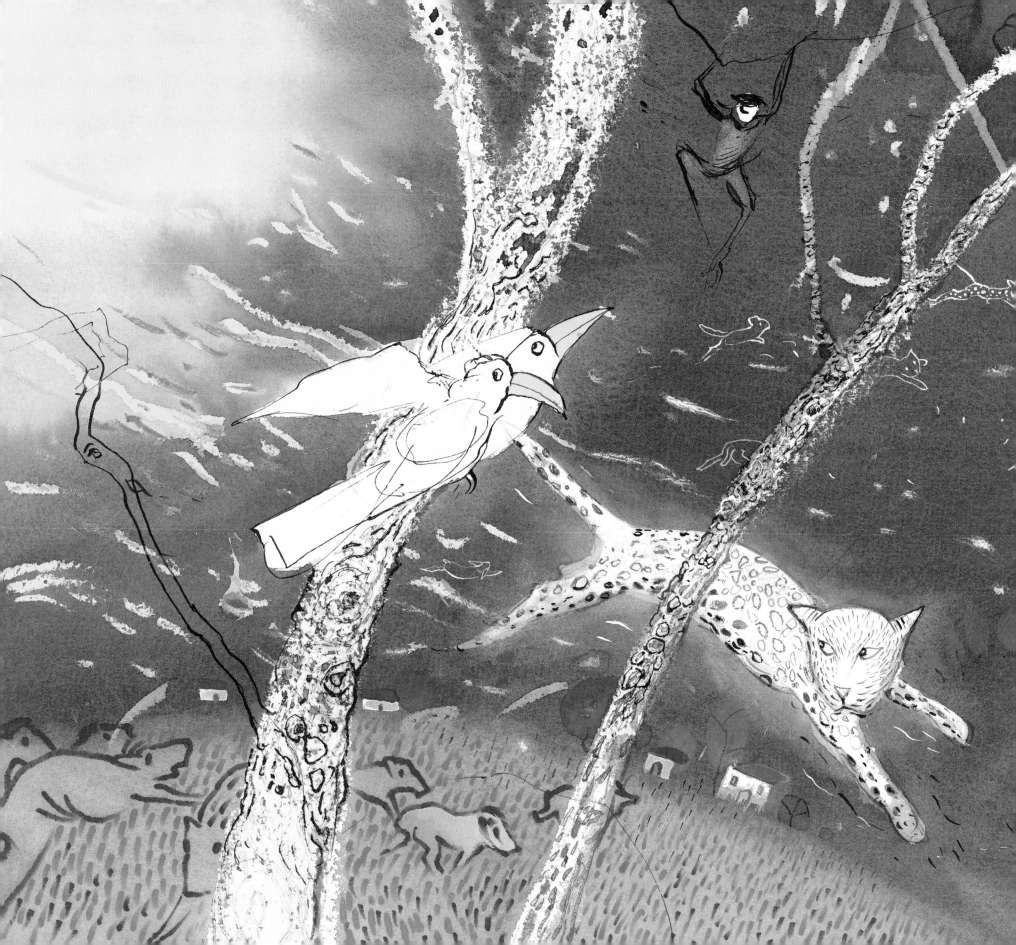

There's a Fire in the Forest

There's a fire in the forest!
The creatures are fleeing
The flames close behind
With the wind driving onward.
From underbrush up to
The high moving tree-tops
The fire's surging forward.
There's a fire in the forest;
The whole woods are burning.
The whole world is burning!

The creatures are seeking
The safety of streams
Beyond the hot burning.
The creatures are fleeing;
They are labouring, straining
To reach the cool river
They know just beyond them,
To escape the fierce burning,
To reach the cool stream
For which they are yearning.

W W E ROSS

Water

Waves crash and then disappear
Giants paddle when no one can hear,
Raindrops race like stars shooting low
Rivers rush with nowhere to go.

Shipwrecks creak down under the sea
Saucepans sizzle just before tea,
Hosepipes hiss like snakes in a spin
Drains gurgle under their skin.

Baths bubble all steaming and hot
Coffee pours out of its pot,
Waterfalls roar to warn you away
Wishing wells wait to hear what you say.

Buckets tip when left by the door
Umbrellas drip onto the floor,
Snowmen melt into the ground
And wellingtons splash like no other sound.

ANDREW COLLETT

37

The Moonwuzo's Song

Who is that walking on the dark sea sand?
The old Bride of the Wind

What is that staring out of the weedy pool?
The newborn Monster in its caul

What is that eerie chanting from the foam?
The Mermaid's gardening song

What is that shadow floating on the water?
The Fish-King's daughter

Who bears those candles down by the Sea's curled rim?
The children going home

CARA LOCKHART SMITH

Old Man Ocean

Old Man Ocean, how do you pound
Smooth glass rough, rough stones around?
Time and the tide and the wild waves rolling.
Night and the wind and the long grey dawn.

Old Man Ocean, what do you tell,
What do you sing in the empty shell?
Fog and the storm and the long bell tolling,
Bones in the deep and the brave men gone.

RUSSELL HOBAN

Haiku

After the storm, wild horses
thunder through tide pools —
their own rain

J PATRICK LEWIS

I Am the Rain

I am the rain
I like to play games
like sometimes
    I pretend
I'm going
    to fall
Man, that's the time
I don't come at all
Like sometimes
I get these laughing stitches
up my sides
    rushing people in
and out
    with the clothesline
I just love drip
    dropping
down collars
    and spines
Maybe it's a shame
but it's the only way
I get some fame

GRACE NICHOLS

40

The Dark Grey Clouds

The dark grey clouds,
the great grey clouds,
the black rolling clouds are elephants
going down to the sea for water.
They draw up the water in their trunks.
They march back again across the sky.
They spray the earth with the water,
and men say it is raining.

TRADITIONAL INDIAN

Think of the Ocean

think of the ocean
    as a cat
with her grey fur
    pushed
    high upon her back
       white boots
      kneading the shore
        on stormy days.

But
    with the sun
        shining
in a silk blue sky
      she purrs
softly and her fur is
      licked smooth and green
like the sand stone
        she sleeps upon.

SIOBHAN SWAYNE

Copyright Acknowledgements

The compiler and publisher would like to thank the following for permission to reprint the poems in this book. All possible care has been taken to trace the ownership of the poems included, and to make full acknowledgement of their use. Any errors or omissions which have accidentally occurred despite these efforts will be corrected in subsequent editions if notification is sent to the publisher.

Page 10 'Earth Song' from *Collected Poems* by Langston Hughes. Copyright © by the Estate of Langston Hughes. Reprinted by permission of Alfred A Knopf Inc. and David Higham Associates Limited

Page 12 'Knowing the Earth' © Nancy Wood, from *Spirit Walker*, Bantam Doubleday Dell, New York 1993. All rights reserved

Page 13 'I Sing for the Animals' by Teton Sioux, reprinted from *The Sky Clears: Poetry of American Indians* by A Grove Day, by permission of the University of Nebraska Press. Copyright 1951 by A Grove Day

Page 16 'I Like the World' taken from *The Day I Fell Down the Toilet and Other Poems* by Steve Turner published by Lion Publishing and reproduced with permission

Page 18 'On Looking into the Grand Canyon' From *The House That Caught Cold* Copyright © Richard Edwards, 1991. Reproduced by permission of Felicity Bryan and the author

Page 21 'The Wind' © Dr Riad Nourallah. Reprinted by permission of the author

Page 24 'Wind Cat' © 1994 The Estate of Robert Westall

Page 28 'Sun' from *All the Small Poems and Fourteen More* by Valerie Worth. Copyright © 1987, 1994 by Valerie Worth. Reprinted by permission of Farrar, Straus and Giroux, LLC